MARBLES IN THE COOKIE JAR

POEMS BY TONY MARINO
A TEACHER-POET

PublishingWorks, Inc.
Exeter, NH
2008

PublishingWorks, Inc.,
60 Winter Street
Exeter, NH 03833
603-778-9883

For Sales and Orders:
1-800-738-6603 or 603-772-7200

Cover design & Photography: Anna Godard

LCCN: 2008930616
ISBN: 1-933002-88-3
ISBN-13: 978-1-933002-88-0

Contents

Acknowledgements

To my wife Diane, my best friend; my son Tony, who pleaded with me to go forward with this project—see Tony's poem on page 78; my daughter Mikelanne, who gave me my grandsons, Nicholas and Cole, and more inspiration to write; to all the great students, teachers, and parents I worked with during my teaching years; to all my family and friends; and a special thank you to the group of librarians who attended my poetry reading at the 2001 Maine Library Conference and encouraged me to share my writing with the world.

FOREWORD

Mr. Marino

One morning quite an event took place
A mother looked down at a cherubic face
She smiled and said, "What a bambino
His name will go down as Tony Marino."

Today he is a real cool cat
With real "big" muscles and such a brat
He likes to play with marbles a lot
But when he's winning he's usually caught

He tries to be a macho guy
But that attempt will always die
Because he's really soft inside
Tony the teacher, our greatest pride.

To Mr. Marino
a great teacher
from Johanna Topitzer
7th grade
Pentucket Middle School
June 1981

Vinny Gillon's Shooter

vinny gillon's shooter
sits in the cookie jar
above my mantle along
with the 869 marbles I've
saved in mrs baralou's gift
from 109 sargent street
how I finally won it is
vague now …
the game we played for keepsies
seemed to splay itself on that
hot dusty day from dingle park or jackson parkway
to the holyoke public library
we battled for hours
with shooters and moonies
tomatoes and bombers
wagering the lowly cat's-eyes
and vinny kept losing
and his once marble-filled pockets
emptied into mine
until only his shooter remained
vinny never knew what hit him
for on that final test of bunny in the hole
his prized shooter
a magnificent multicolored
slighty off-centered master
of the shooter stop
popped in the hole that
sunny day so long ago
and landed in my cookie jar
as vinny marble empty
slowly walked away
i'll give it back to you vinny
some day
i promise

Thanksgiving

it comes to me every Thanksgiving
a dream of baking pies and roasting beasties
my mom with her magic hands cooking
and peeling with carrots and turnips
potatoes and stuffing
both meat and bread
we rose from our beds to the fragrance of the
holiday-turkey day again
i sat at the formica table a potato peeler in hand
with my sisters Barbara and Ann and Terry and Mary
and little Donna too
we'd lose ourselves in a sea of vegetables
as the peels flew through the air
and mingled with the giggles and the aromas
that come to me every Thanksgiving
football and cool crisp air
polka music on the radio
hustle was everywhere
a big table for the grownups
small cardboard for the kids
the kitchen shined from the fourth floor
atop a brick building lost in the city
our tiny home encased in streets and crisscrossing alleyways
Thanksgiving morning and the world was turkey-filled and warm
with the oven bursting with breads and blue-black pans
and mom was everywhere at once
like the magician she moved
so quick her hands whirled away at
the business of the day
and dad would lean across the countertop
carving small sculptures from Idaho potatoes
his stubble beard ready to scrape our cheeks

and squeeze us silly
109 sargent street, holyoke, massachusetts
eight apartments filled with people
with us close to the sky stuffed
in the kitchen
drenched with love and Thanksgiving
smells and music and laughter and turkey
and stuffing and turnip and squash and
mom
with her magic hands and her magic smile …
it comes to me every Thanksgiving
all the way from holyoke
straight from 109 sargent street
the message
from the pilgrims
on the fourth floor
Happy Thanksgiving

Hopscotch

I took the chalk from my sister's drawer
and ran down the stairs
straight to the pavement
hopscotch blocks
bits of colored glass
our tickets in

I'd toss my tiny glass
and hop my path one-legged
hopscotch
and chalk was everywhere
poor blueprints
here on the city street
yet the hours filled our days
we lept canyons
crossed the highest peaks
teetered on the line of death
hopscotch
with bits of colored glass
our tickets out
to make believe

Holyoke Halloween

It was a deep dark
chocolatey delicious night
little goblins squeaked and
shuffled through the
paper bag night
tiny little hands knocked on
huge brown wooden doors
and big hands and little hands
and old hands and pretty hands
dropped little sweet
scrumdelicious things that settled to the
bottom of our bags
and the bags got ever so heavy
and the candy got ever so sweet
that we ran out of houses
and tried unknown streets and
said names on the doors that we couldn't read
and couldn't say
in neighborhoods we never knew
and our tiny little feet
shuffled through the deep dark
halloweeny night so long
ago in the dark dark
streets of neighborhoods
filled with candy
and tricks or treats
and soapy waxy windows
long ago when i was just a tiny little goblin
with lipstick on my face

Snow

I make a deep cave

In the snow

To hide away

Alone and cold

And alone …

I like my cave

I dug it with my fingers

The frost is on my mittens

And my nose

Is running

As usual.

Novena with Mom

It started with the sound
Of the pitter-patter
Of my head against the pillow
My heartbeat becomes my footsteps
As I jump the last three stairs
On the wooden porches
Behind our apartment
Pitter-patter
my sneakers
Move along stopping at the back
Of the churchill club to grab
Some loose change from someone
Sleeping it off
Past robert's market
And bill's fishing supply
Straight to sacred heart church
To the pew four rows from the front
Pitter-patter pitter
I genuflect and slide
Ceremoniously close to my mom
That dark beautiful figure wearing
The black veil
Pitter-patter pitter
Our week of worship comes to an end
Just the two of us ...
Surely now we will go
Straight to heaven together

The Poetry Monster

the poetry monster
came into my bed
last night
he brought me people
from my past
my mom who combed
my hair again
arranged my rosary beads
and first communion book
my dad to scrape my
cheek with his stubble beard
they tickled my toes and
pinched my ears
i felt the warm hand
on my shoulder and knew
it was my father-in-law
and there was grandpa suds rowing his rented boat
across hampton ponds
to give me a sip of his beer
don't forget to spit on your worm poopy legs
baby michael anthony came too …
whispering i miss you … where have i been?
strange how they come like that
in the middle of my dreams
these people from my past
who love me still
bruising me
so silent
into my bed
late at night

Obituaries

my father could have been a mortician
a mad one at that
he read the obituaries
every day
the first section he turned to
in the local newspaper
I am very sorry for your troubles
my obsessive obituarion
maybe some day i will cut
them into tiny little
pieces—these microbial death notices
with a pair of tiny little scissors
and bring them to my stepladder
and simply blow them
in a veiled shower onto my compost pile
i'm very sorry for your troubles
as he filled his notebook
name age church calling hours
predeceased by a brother or sister
survived by his loving wife of 60 years
sons and daughters
beloved grandchildren
and three great grandchildren
and several nieces and nephews
contributions can be made to …
thoughts and prayers offered
i am truly sorry for your troubles
smith thursday Mater Delarosa 6–8 pm
an avid gardener
larson weds Sacred Heart calling hrs 4–6 pm
loved to crochet
worked on church bazaars
past tense past prime past.
the rising sun

obituaries scissored from your
newsaper sorted by day
and date and calling hours
"very sorry for your trouble"
he would have loved this crowd
she loved to sing
volunteered at crossroads house
served in the marine corps in wwII
worked at the naval yard in portsmouth
retired in 1978 ... past tense
loved to cook and bake and peel
and dice and chop and mix
and make pizza faces with
pepperoni eyes and black olive smiles
beloved husband and father
spoiled his grandchildren
spending time at his lakeside camp
fishing ... dreaming
o'leary weds Holy Cross Church 3–5 & 6–8pm
always loved corned beef and cabbage
and green beer and st. patrick's day
marino tuesday Santa Lucias 6–8pm
loved to read the obituaries

Poker Night

the uncles shared the cards
it might have been a five card stud hand
the beers the peanuts
the raucous laughter
uncle dan the holyoke cop
uncle bill the school custodian
my boyhood heroes
enjoying another poker night
until i barged in
a bleary-eyed college boy
screaming at my father
something about bills and money
and overdue rent
i deserved the beer you threw in my face
as mom cringed in the corner
hiding her tears pretending to
talk to the parakeet
uncle frank never told me about his tour in the phillipines
i read about it in his obituary
what must you have thought
of me that night uncle frank
could you ever forgive me
for busting up your poker time together
all you had to do dad was to hold me
and tell me you loved me
uncle louie uncle dan uncle frank
uncle bill uncle renny uncle ernest
i can still smell the camels and the hampden beer
you were my holyoke heroes
"my deal, five card stud
five ten fifteen
deuces and one eyed jacks wild
ante up boys"

"Daddy," You Said

November 1, 1976

"Daddy," you said with the stars all around and the moon
peering down through thick halloweeny skies.
"Daddy," you said, "I wish we could stay just the
way we are now. I wish we could have life forever.
You and me and Mikey and Mommy with all the
people in the world.
Just the way we are now … forever."
So I picked you up and found your face full of questions
and innocent childhood dreams looking up at me.
I held you close and kissed your cheek and whispered,
"I wish that you could stay like this my little boy
so I could hold your little body next to mine
and touch your golden hair
and wind-swept face."
And then I pressed my cheek close to you and smelled
your bubble gum world, your little boy smell
that only little boys can have.
And I felt the wrinkle of your new winter coat
and the warmth of your knitted cap.
I squeezed your little body and said, "But you can't stay little
cause you have to grow and live
and stretch your body tall.
You have to change and be a man someday.
But I'll watch you through the windows
of my eyes and try to share with you.
I'll be there to hope for you and stand beside you
if you need me."
"But most of all my little boy,
here in the dark cloud-filled November night,
most of all, I don't want you to change
I want you here with me
Here in the darkness unnoticed,
Here alone forever.
For you are the part of my being
that holds the puzzle parts of me together
and when you go …"

"Yes my little boy, I too wish we could stay
just the way we are now. I wish we
could have life forever. You and me and Mikey
and Mommy with all the people in the world.
Just the way we are now ... forever."

Evie's Story
October 16, 1975

i walked out into the autumn sun and rainbow-colored trees
and fresh air helped to clear away the things i'd left inside the
school
and for a moment i forgot the chalkdust-filled rooms
and the punishments …
i walked away to my waiting car and felt reborn
just a little
cause i left behind the crumpled papers and the surging
life-infested hallways
and i left with my usual kaleidoscope of kids
peering and shouting …
and i left behind some kids with magic moments
and some who couldn't wait to leave
and i came home through highways filled with sunshine
and i felt real warm inside …
just enough to get me home
i walked in the house and my little girl
came my way with her story-filled day
and i was just about to hide behind my nightly newspaper
when i glanced up and saw her mouth opening and closing
and then i saw the tears in her eyes … so i sat up
and began to listen and i heard her say
"Daddy there's a little girl in my room named Evie.
And she has a pushed in nose and everyone picks on her."
I looked up and asked, "Mikey do you ever pick on her?"
and my little blond-haired flower answered, "I used to Daddy
but I stopped because I thought that if I was Evie
and all the kids called me names and pushed me around,
I'd cry and be very lonely …"
"Hey Mikey," I said, "you make me feel real good inside."
and she looked at me and stared and said, "But Christine
teased Evie today and Evie was crying and I told Christine
to stop teasing her. And how would she like to be teased and
cry all the time.

-14-

and Christine said, 'Well I'm not Evie, so there!' So Daddy
I played with Evie and I feel real bad that I called
her names and made her cry and I'll never do it
again ever."
and i sat there and swallowed an empty swallow and bit
my lip and reached down and kissed my little blond-haired
girl and i told her again and again, "I love you.
Mikey—I really, really love you."
and i felt real warm inside i mean really, really warm
and we both looked at each other and started laughing and
crying at the same time
and i felt a tear and looked at my little girl and we
laughed and cried together for the first time ever
and i knew that me and Mikey would never
be the same again … ever.

Jumping Rope

I just finished jumping rope with my little girl
We jumped to "I like coffee, I like tea"
In a rain-drenched chorus of giggles
And "Daddy jump in"

We jumped together in loving time
Until our eyes met
And the rain-soaked cheeks
And the happy-coated eyes
screamed out to me, Daddy, it's madness
It's crazy and I love you"

But that was yesterday, my dear
And in some faraway tomorrow
When I'm old and wrinkled
With your child on my knee
I'll look your way and ask
"Hey Mikey, remember the time
We jumped rope in an April shower?"

And we two will jump rope again
And like some teetering tightrope walker
I'll think of you and know
A tiny bit of me, a mitosis of myself
Flew off to unknown artistry
To sculpt a memory of me

Chestnut Acre Farm

I thought of you again
my son
we fed the sheep one more time
and said goodnight
to our favorite laying hens
clucking as they perched on their roosts
checking one last time
for recent eggs
as I shut out the world
and think only of you
back on that dark November night
when we wandered Chestnut Acre Farm
while the world raged
beyond our tiny pasture
won't you please come back
and take our favorite egg basket
from my hand
and share with me one more trip
to the sleepy-filled barn
on what we once called
our Chestnut Acre Farm

Cardinals in Winter

thanks to the four-
pound bag of special birdseed mix
a cardinal has graced our
winter yard with
his mate
several times this winter
stopping to clear the coast of cats
and hidden hawks
they make a pretty pair
those two red and brilliant
in the sunlight he stands
to guard his
quiet mate
quickened eyes
and crunching beak
he watches
to soothe the fear
of his close red friend
they come a lot
to sit on the snow near the kitchen window
sharing the winter with us

Asparagus

the asparagus
rush to meet
the warming sun
bent from the rocky soil
they kick and claw
to the surge of spring
silent stalks
sweet-nurtured from
trench-deep beginnings
I soften the topsoil
to ease their journey
spring showers cool them
quench the long winter's thirst
some bent
beyond repair
return to their beginnings
others so splendid their
magnificence grows
before your eyes as
slow as worms
but at a fever pitch
slow and rapid
green gargoyles
they trumpet forth
the garden song
harbingers of spring
from earth's womb
yielding another year's harvesting
coming slow
leaving far too soon

Mockingbird

how strange you looked
surrounded by songbirds mocking you
chickadees warblers blue jays
how strange to see you locked
in my have-a-heart-trap
without a song of your own
did the woodchuck come to mock you too
how silly you must feel
there among the peanut buttered apple slices
through the asparagus stalks
your cage for the moment
perhaps this is your fascination each spring
as you mark and mock your territory
as song sparrows seek other nesting sites
sly mockingbird
how silent and silly you must feel
you who knows every bird song but your own
if you only had a voice
speak—tell your tale of woe …
i release you now—
find your voice my mockingbird friend

Fences Come and Go

once strung to hold
spring lambs
now, it lies
a simple roll
of sheep fencing
to be cooly stored
at one dark corner of the barn
fences come and go
stretched to the lower field
to fit rotation
first here
then the far field
and, to my ultimate delight
the field close to the road
and passersby stop to
catch a glimpse of this
spring's newborn lambs,
in lilac time
purples, white, and pink
and pink-tongued baby lambs
suckled rich with ewe's milk
provide a glorious spring
but fences mostly go now
soon the perimeter will remain alone
the lambs, the ewes, the singular ram
all gone …
not hay, nor water, or the molasses-scented
salt lick remain
the fences came and went
the pasture turns to groomed lawn
the fences come and go
like long-lost friends

Seagulls

The seagulls
stood like
sentinels

on the shore

staring out
at the white
foam fury
of the sea

strange

they hardly
noticed me
standing there

in the winter
wind
with them

on christmas eve

staring
all of us
out to sea

awaiting

in the seaweed swirl
and broken shells

sentinels by the sea

on christmas eve

The Snow Fort

i went to the abandoned
snow fort left
near the road by the
neighborhood kids
i dug myself a path
fit for
a king and
traveled through the passages to china
and the king's best treasure
room
it was all so fascinating
there hidden in the snow
room after room
of military might
a storehouse of frozen snowballs
and secret compartments
etched in frozen snow
windows and sliding snow-covered doors
with kings and princes
politicians and occasional running
snow water
i was only four snow prints from the front door
and my mother called me for dinner
while I hid in the white castle
near the kingdom of the snow god

The Goldfish

the goldfish in our
fish tank
keeps staring
at me
and waving his tail
he tilts his head
just so
to sniff the air
up
he floats
and down again
enmeshed in plastic plants
and staring
glass-stained fish eyes
he sends me a riddle
"I swim too"

"You Won't Find Treasure Here"

"you won't find treasure here,"
 said the chickadee.
"you were warned not to come too close to
 the world of the winter birds
 weren't you told to stay inside
 with your self-contained
 hidden heat and storehouse
 of january meals
 stay inside we chorused to the
 wind off the winter sea
 somebody tell this guy
 he's not a bird
 and can never hope to fly with us or
 huddle in the naked chill
 of the elm tree down the street
 you wouldn't make it in the world of the
 birds
 anyway chum
 you have no place to nurture wings or
 perch your heart upon the snow
 no, you won't find treasure here,
 'tis well that you can sit and watch us
 struggle here at the feeder for
 tiny seeds tossed in the snow …
 no treasure here …"

Cross Stitch—The Dragon

i watch you there
on the couch
glasses propped up on your nose
skeins of multi-colored thread
cascading to the floor
stitch stitch stitch
"you write poetry too"
and your tiny needle work
ever so slowly takes the shape
of a whimsical dragon
"how much left?"
I ask.

"Oh just his foot and the border
and the mat
i think I'll use a dark wooden frame."

how i love to watch you work
and create to please the eye
of some stranger
in a strange library
i love to watch you in your little
cross stitch world
making a dragon for the world
"you write poetry too"

Kids You Should Have Been There

My Memorial Day Poem
Dedicated to the Kids at Pentucket

You really should have been there
In the middle of the night
The rockets screeched in terror
Over bodies wrong or right

You really should have been there
In a foxhole on the beach
The guns spit forth their message
Seeking eyes and hearts to reach

You could have seen a soldier
Hold his buddy as he died
And maybe watched his sweetheart
As she read the news and cried

You could have watched from mountain tops
And seen a sea of blood
You could have seen our blood-scarred soldiers
Dying in the mud

The children too you would have seen
Playing tag among the bombs
And tiny little babies
Searching madly for their moms

And maybe if you had the time
To sit and really stare
You'd wonder why the death and pain
Could be so damn unfair

Yes, you really should have been there
When they fought to keep us free
You might have seen our armies
As they marched in misery

Yes kids, you should have been there
It's really quite a shame
Cause if you could have seen it
You'd never be the same

And now we blow the bugle
And fold the flag with pride
We stare ino each other's eyes
Feeling warm and good inside

For those who fought with sword and shield
Didn't really want you there
I think that they'd be happy
Just knowing that you care

No, those who fought the battles
Did not want you to see
I think that they are quite content
That you and I are free

Ball of Clay

They handed me a ball
        Of clay
Plopped it on my desk
        And said
"Here, try to make something
          out of this!"
the shapeless mass
      slowly spread
a crude map upon
       my desk
I pounced upon
       The seeping glob
And slowly formed a shape
       To please my eyes
A polished edge
     A mountain turned to tunnel
And slowly …
       Emerged
        As if cast in an age of stone
A replica
   Fused in gold
     A tiny princess
   Come back to life;
  Each tiny ridge
    And curve
Spake clearly of the sculptor's plight
  And golden eyes
 Drew history
   And the tiny princess
  Began to fill the
    Thirsty chalice
  As suckled youth to fill the void
Left empty on my bludgeoned desk
The pilgrimage brought strangers

In their last attempt at truth
As doubters doubting gracefully
        To seek some secret
                Of themselves
And not once did the princess smile,
        Or nod her head of clay,
But simply stood on golden legs
    On a woodworn desk
    Until her golden smile
        In dying candle death became
                A ball of clay
            Plopped on my desk
As thousands tore the shredded mass
To pulp
    To steal a piece of truth
And the air was heard
        To sob in a voice
            So very like
                The song of some
                    Segmented princess
                        Who'd wandered much too far

Chapter 766: The Sunshine Kids

They come in all sizes and shapes
some on wooden legs
some in silver chairs on rolling wheels
if you see them
you feel a heavy thud in your heart
for they leave you with a picture of faces full of sunshine
and hearts full of hope
a picture painted with wonder and love
for they move in beauty as they plod their way
as others run to carry on the
business of empty childhood
they move so alone amidst the skipping
and empty giggling
if you speak their way you feel the weight
of early years
you grasp the burden of wasted tears
for when you see them among the crowd
with staring, pitying eyes
they seem so all alone
But a silent secret awaits you
for their plodding trial has brought
with it a something
A something as elusive as the
dying withering rainbow
for the Sunshine Kids hold the unlocked message
of what awaits the crowd
they know the pain and sorrow
they've dreamed the dream of
a thousand sleepless nights
for the Sunshine Kids are all of us and more
and they and we are
blind and mute and friendless
and they have begged for food
and lost loved ones

they are the universal pain
the lost child
the saddened soldier
these and more … much more
My Sunshine Kids have been the frenzied epileptic
the cancer-ridden father
the empty family
they have born the agony
of lost love and broken dreams
these and more … much more
for the Sunshine Kids are the conscience
of us all
the holy mother and the blessed son
Yes, my little Sunshine Children you're
not just kids on wooden legs
or rolling wheels
Oh, no you kids are more than that … much more
for me and for us all
for every time I look at you
I'm all at once
the everyman …
the every pain … the every hate
and every love the world has yet to nurture
for you and your strength
your urge to be
to love
and be loved
is like a flight of a thousand
frightened sparrows
for no one understands it … no one knows
the reason why
it just is …
And so are you my Sunshine Kids
my inner light
the ones I look to when I feel

i can't go on
for when I feel I've lost my way
just at that magic moment
my inner light
my Sunshine Kids
show me the way
for I see you so warm
and glowing
and strong
and you turn together
and stretch your wooden legs
and roll your chairs on wheels
and fight to walk and plod and smile
but you hurt and you cry ...
but you never stop
no, you'll never ... ever stop
It's then I look at me
and at us all
and feel so empty
humbly I pick up the pieces
and chase your message
Oh, my little Sunshine Children
you'll never really know
what you give me
each day
No, you will never ever know ... never

CB Charlie

charlie do you remember
the story i wrote
for you in 7th grade
about cb charlie
he had no friends
just his good ol' buddies
on the CB radio waves
that was about you
you were cb charlie
sitting silently in the
back of my room trying
to remain anonymous
why didn't you raise
your hand and ask for help
how could you
let your parents find you
hanging in your closet
like an old winter coat
dangling like a christmas ornament
the three wise men
and the little brown boy
bearing gifts for the
baby in a manger
oh, charlie you should have
called me we could have gone
to church together
a week long novena
to discover your demons
sit here in front of the
room right next to me …
keep my desk extra neat
pass out the journals when i tell you
and check our supply
of canada mints
don't let my coffee
thermos tip over
and pour me a cup

occaisionally please
charlie
my cb charlie
you are now and forever duly
appointed my teacher's pet
responsible for being
my left arm man
always at my side
always smiling
always talking to me
spilling out your
deepest darkest secrets
hoping to rescue you forever
from your silent dark side
breaker 19 this is mr marino
to cb charlie
time to pass out the journals
pour me some coffee
and tend to the
canada mints
do you read me?
do you read me?
charlie … charlie …

Cerebral Dominance
My right hemisphere

There is a forest deep in the woods
The trees there are purple and yellow
The birds there sing silent songs
And no one seems to want to listen
The tiny streams are dull broken mirrors
They wind crooked ignorant paths

There is a forest hidden deep within the woods
Where hues seem melted in waxpaper shrouds
The tiny bugs here rule the dirt
With cacophonic minstrels
Their shouts in the night
      In the deep dark forest
         Scatter memories

In the forest in the deep woods are special secrets
Where colors make dreams come true
And feathered warblers orchestrate
      The song of nightingales
In the forest hidden deep within the woods
the colors weep on empty easels
the birds screech choking chirps
and insect armies crawl to carrion
to quarrel in a war
that's hidden
in a forest
hidden deep within the woods

Lunch

it happened at lunch time
i was alone in my room
at my desk piled high with books
there was no grease upon my fingers
just a hint of chalk and ink
and
then I was the gingerbreadman
run away
to meet the faces I would meet
a round one to encircle me
square ones to scrape at me
and even then there came a triangle
whose height was more than
twice my base

and with him too a rhombus
to rough my shying skin
and like some lost
galactic storm of stars
they came at me as if from hell
with maddened pace
octa hexa septa quadra
nona deca dodeca gon
and gon
and gone!
missles at me
this man of startch
this man of ginger and bread
sitting at his desk
in his room
alone
with books piled high
at lunch time

In Search Of

secrets I one day
wandered through a cloudless
time seeking answers
and everywhere were bottomless
pits and nameless streets

in search of
i wandered …
seeking
finding only
that my own
answers
must suffice

If I Weren't a Human Being

my life would be so simple
i'd plug myself into
a convenient outlet
or fill my being at some
high octaned hose
the rest would be so easy
i'd follow a machine mentality
and never miss a step
i'd drown myself in people things
without a hint of hate
or love
or jealousy
why I'd be computed
to be calculated
to be error free
a techno-humo-tomaton
of buzzers and buttons
and lights without view
there'd be no room for error in me
without mind
or heart
or soul
if I weren't a human being
my only fear would be
an unexpected end
as some stupid human being
let mind
or heart
or soul
rage unchecked

Marmalade Man

I am a
man of
marmalade
spread me on your toast
cap the jar
and place me on
your shelf
i come in most flavors
and may stick to your knife
and stain your
fingers orange
i am sweet
and scented
and sticky
in my pliable condition
you may mold my
shape at your will
i could be a map
of china
or a cute lollipop tree
spread me on your
kitchen table and there
on your formica easel
paint with me
your marmalade medium
a shape to please
your eyes
whatever you do
make me pretty!
for i don't feel
so good today

Circles in the Sand

he told me to try
to understand
to open my wings to you
one last time
draw a circle
in the sand he said
and you in your
circle might find
it easier
to see our two circles
more clearly
as simply circles in the sand
it seems a lot easier now
etched in a sand dune
there is no fire of hate
no loud words
no messy emotion …
just two circles
in the sand
and the sandy grains
that keep us apart
are such tiny
tiny
things

Kids on Bent Elbows

look my way

with empty faces

and the message

reads …

the morning came

too soon

and spring seems

so far away

Halloween Grinch

once upon a midnight dreary
ghosts and goblins make me weary
i hate witches I hate cats
i hate owls and flying bats
i eat kids for trick or treat
i eat their brain I chew their feet
i don't give candy I don't give gum
i kick trick or treaters in the bum
i hate the dark I hate the moon
i pray the sun will come out soon
i'm not a witch I'm not a ghoul
i think the little brats should be in school
they shouldn't get tricks or fattening treats
they should get spinach and home-cooked beets
they shouldn't be in costume they should be home in bed
if I had my way I'd hit them in the head
forget halloween the ghosts and witches too
keep the kids at home give them homework to do
no more candy no more fun at night
keep them all at home keep them out of sight
put them in their squeaky beds shut them up for good
let parents trick or treat around the neighborhood
why should kids get all the treats why should they be happy
halloween should be for grownups your mommy and your
pappy

Another Poem About the End of School

would be so appropriate
and yet I don't know where to begin
shall I begin with the constant buzzing
of kids drilling me with meaningless questions
or shall I begin with the daily barrage of
do's and don'ts
don't do this and do do that
don't shout
don't fight
don't throw food in the cafeteria
don't stick your gum under the desk
don't talk back
do your homework
do your best
dress like a human being
don't be a slob
don't run in the halls
don't tell lies
don't swear
detention
suspension
retention
expulsion!

A Poetry Friend

a poetry friend
shapes the sky
and fondles the
frightened sparrow

a poetry friend is
the painter's canvas
and the chisel in
the sculptor's arm

my friend makes suns
smile and turns
rainbows into ribbons

a poetry friend
comes with a warming
phrase or mellows me
with silent stares

a poetry friend is another you
a part of you who listens
and understands
yet is quite content
to smile
and share your smiles

Don't Throw Away Old Poems

cause when you do
you throw away
a part of me
and you
and him
and her
and them that thought
they knew you
and them that felt the warmth of you
you throw away your soul
the soul you never saved
you cleave the star
that never shined
no, never throw away a poem
that started as a spark
and became a lump
in your throat
you could flush them
or burn them
or shred
or rip them apart
but don't … please don't
for when you do …
you eliminate a part of you

Poetry Exchanges

poetry exchanges
as you passed
me in the hall
slipped it in my shirt pocket
or in a page in my journal
sometimes so secret
folded neatly
signed and dated
name and date and division
i told you that
every day
poetry exchanges
while on duty in the caf
something about your mother
and your cat
poetry exchanges
could make my day
soar above the
punishment assignments
the faculty meetings
how easily your words
would erase it all
I've kept them all
you know
in boxes in the attic
year by year
school by school
name and date
and division
i read them at times and your words
still tear at me
they haunt me still
these poetry exchanges
hoping once more to reach into
my pocket and
find one neatly
folded …

for me to read again
poetry exchanges
stuffed in the attic
with my son's tonka trucks
i still look for you
in the hallway outside room 107

Poetry Wives

fear not the
poetry wives
oblivious to our
turmoiled lives
and blood red
metered eyes

they pass us by
day after day
tossing poems
into garbage bags

like so many unpaid bills
and long lost recipes

how misunderstanding they
to be so aloof and
full of today

not feeling the pain
and the
shame
as we pour our
souls out
in lines never
written
in thoughts never
thought

how strange
to have my moonlight
yearnings tossed
aside with the
morning marmalade
and last month's tv guide

Funeral Plans

First day of spring

i am going to take your poems
to the grave with me
I've decided
while driving furiously
down atlantic avenue
and a poem comes my way …
Write it down …
You'll forget—
it's the poetry monster
whispering in my ear
write me write me
yes i will take my attic poems
my student poems
that I've collected
over the years
i will take them
with me when i die
i will shred them
into a funeral shroud
ask that this poetic blanket
be placed in my coffin
to cushion me in my
eternal rest
yes, your voices
and hearts and tears
and hugs will be with me through eternity
no i will never forget you
and i will hear your
words until the
end of time
i stopped at little river salt marsh
to pen this poem
please don't forget me as soon
as i am gone
forever wrapped in the warmth of your words
i can still see you smiling sometimes.

Love is Blind

love is blind
and stupid
and mute

it is lungs without breath
fire without ember
soul without sin
love is madness
of the mind
a craziness that claws us
to unspeakable ends

a turtle out of shell
a scream without sound
my heart without beat
my love without you

I Wrote a Poem Once

I wrote a poem once
one poem
it seemed like
it never would
happen again
but it did

and there it was
a poem
something new
words in unison
as never before

i wrote a poem
once
and there it
stood
for just a minute

and then it fell flat
on its face
when i looked a second time

I Won't Write About

i won't write
about
winter
it's much too cold
and raw
and uninviting
at least from here
out on the lawn
piled high with snow
and ice
and squirrel
footprints
i could tell where
you stopped to dig
for hidden
treasure in the snow
with your bushy grey tail
signaling
the sun to shine
along the fence row
digging frantically
for the hidden womb
of spring

Hiding

there's a poem somewhere

hiding

waiting to be written

the lines are ready

verses primed

an alphabetical mosaic

locked away

in a room

somewhere

cowering from

the poet's stare

Chronology

we are weaned
as bubbles in a
soft drink float
to open air

our umbilical beginnings
become a forfeit love
affair
with mothers who
never loved

scars shaped serpents
hairs greyed and
skin's velvet touch
turned hands to
wrinkled mushrooms

days and nights fought
the terror of clock
and bright eyes
faded to furrowed jewels
spines bent and mouths
marched a murderous cadence

until the mirror shouted
back in easel-white
that life had slipped
us by

I Drill a Hole in My Head

i drill a hole

in my head

within

i go

deeper

deeper

and peer inside

stepping into my cranium

i begin my journey

slipping through neuron endings

falling over dendrites

and grey tissue

i look for tell tale signs

a discoloration

a tiny distortion

some vague sign of damage

to explain my frantic ways

Sleepwalkers

tissue paper dreams
kaleidoscope my sight
the worms crawled in
to spend the night

a dozen sleepwalkers
crowd my room
some with plastic smiles
one was on a broom

some wore hats of clay
others dressed in red
one a crown of thorns
shadows of the dead

when out in the yard
there arose such a clatter
i jumped from my window
and hit the ground with a splatter

Snow Princess

strange
how they found him
dead
in his cave under
the snow
with his heart gone
the snow princess
left her mark
in tiny crimson footprints
on her path
back to winter mountain
strange though
lying there
heaped in red
in the white snow
without his heart
strange …
he smiles so

She Moved So Quickly

you couldn't see her hands
we knew there were tricks
but no one could see her secrets
mad magician
rivers turned to ribbons
before our eyes
no trap doors
no hidden bunnies
just a magic …
a power …
and there I was
dancing
giggling …
rosy cheeked
a marionette
and she controled the strings
and me
clip clop …
cut out the heart
and drill a hole in me
open the lungs
breath to me
split the skull
implant the brain
treat me as you will
yet bestow
your glee
paint your eccentricity
dress me well
with shoes down to the
touch of costume
and when satisfied
that I've become your servant
and I will serve thee well
touch my hand as only
you can do
and fly with me

your wooden me
fly with me
and make me sense
the you I cannot see
for now
the puppet me
with strings and painted cheek
and clumsy costume
will scratch
my wooden head
and wonder at the
heart beat in
the pine of me

The Calling
Pope John Paul I

"Hey paul, how's it going?"

"I'm worried.
      I don't think i
         can handle it."

"Don't worry about it.
            Come with me."

"Thank God!"

"Never mind that, just
      come with me."

10 oct 78

The Furnace

with
its steady hum
shakes the house
every so often
as the flame ignites
and gallons of
oil rush to
unexpected death
in the fires in the cellar
of my winter home
unsuspecting
liquid red hot death
to warm the cold
awaiting furniture,
the aging bones
hidden here every weekend
away from the toil
of the week's work
closed in the home we
make and heat
and struggle to
keep clean
and full of love
while winter wails away just
beyond the door

Salvatore Salmonella Gambolini

two eggs sunny side up
just one more time
maybe with a slice of canadian bacon
hey can i order some over easy here
salvatore finds
his slippers in their usual place beside his hospital bed
the rubber sheet entwines him
as he stretches to reach his wheelchair
the green and gold logo
of the wentworth village elder care
greets him again with a sad smile
hey sunny side up today
with some whole wheat toast
for christ sakes
one more dip into the simmering sea
into the soft sunny-side-up yellow yolk
one dip of his toes
into the churning sea
he dreams the dream
of a thousand sun-splashed chardonnay cheers
slowly he sleeps dreaming of his lost love
and his long lost youth
and they walk again their property
along the concrete patio
by the honeysuckle
and her favorite perennial sunflowers
he swoons in his sleep and dreams the dream
over and over again
two eggs sunny side up
whole wheat toast and garlic-flavored butter
salvatore salmonella gambolini
sleep old man sleep
and please wipe that egg yolk
from your silly smiling chin
he presses her wedding band
into his brittle vein-carved hand
his hands so pale and white

getting whiter very day
soon he will disappear
a piece of white
just a soft indenture
on the nursing home sheets
his last mark on the world
until the nurse makes the bed again
"look he's sleeping in his wheelchair again....
strange how he smiles so...."

The Silly Old Fool Goes to School

i saw a crossing guard today
i think his name was Willy
i wanted to go back to school ok
and be completely silly

i wanted to be a bad boy
i wanted you folks to really see
how wicked and naughty
this silly old fool could be

so on the way to school today
i sat in the back of the bus
i drank a beer and smoked a butt
i created an absolute fuss

i ran into the principal's office
and gave him a pretty pink rose
and when he turned to look at it
i punched him right in the nose

and then i went to art class
and painted it black and blue
that fuddy-duddy teacher
didn't quite know what to do

then i took off for lunch
and ran to the cafeteria
i started throwing sloppy joes
causing quite a big hysteria

i kissed the girls and chased them
and made them gasp for air
one of them was quite upset
so i put marshmallow in her hair

and then i went to my gym class
with a cherry on my nose
i ran around the whole time
not wearing any clothes

i checked in with the nurse's office
i brought my little pet mouse
and when she wasn't looking
i dropped it in her blouse

the bell rang and the kids ran
to the bus which wasn't very far
so i sat in my seat with my feet up
and lit up a big cigar

i know this sounds preposterous
and really quite absurd
especially the goofy things
you boys and girls just heard

so i was the old fool who went to school
and created quite a scene
but i know that when i wake up
it will all be a silly dream.

Quick Take My Coat ...

I think I will read something for inspiration
Maybe something from shakespeare
Or robert frost "whose woods these are I think I know"
Or something from parade magazine about pomegranates

No I think I'll read something from the old man
With the diamond earring
Something about cardinals or crows
Or maybe kids writing poetry screaming I love you
No I'll read about my dad
And my five sisters
No I think I'll read about my mom
And how much I love her
And how much I miss her
And wish I could hold her hand
Again one last time
One last time to huddle
In her rocking chair
And tell her I love her again and again
Just to sit in her lap and rock and rock
And rockedy-do again
And again and again forever

Quick give me back my coat
I think I've said too much
I've written far too much
I've gone much too far

Crow Commotion

crows on the lawn
and your former
feathered friends
picked at your eyes
as your blood mixed
with the morning dew
on the groomed lawn
of the mansion
by the sea
how odd amidst
the beauty of a new hampshire
seashore morning
to see you
slaughtered there in the shade
humbled onto the grass
begging to be saved
like some corpse
in the boxcars
at Dachau
we're no different
than the crows ...

The Teepee
September 12, 2001

i talked to a chickadee
at my thistle feeder
this morning
curious how comforting
these little creatures
can be at times
after running crazed
through the dying sunflower stalks
kicking mad at dahlias
finding only rage
in the usual serenity
of my backyard
weeping ... weeping
until I found
my little chickadee
feasting on thistle
soothing so soothing
i walk back to the garden
and crawl into my grandson nicholas'
pole bean-draped teepee
sitting silently on the straw-matted floor
crying wishing nicholas
was here with me ... safe
in our teepee ...
far away from what
men do to men

To Our Grandsons

The day will come
when we will pass these
precious treasures on to you
The great grandfather clock
chiming out a song to you every half-hour
grammy's cross stitch collection
of hearts and santa clauses
granpy's ancient cookie jar
filled with all those dusty marbles
great grammy's antique silverware
the paintings around the house
you've loved for so long
you never met the artist great granpy Larry
he would have loved you so
the treasured toys from your mom and uncle tony
preserved for you in the attic
the yearbooks, high school jackets
my hockey skates and pads
grammy's faded white figure skates
tiny treasures—like my favorite
red swiss army knife
our special box of crayons and our coloring book collection
yes we will pass them all on to you
the day will come
sooner rather than later
to always remind you
of grammy and granpy marino

April Morning

We are the pajama clad gardeners
Toiling to sweep away the
Remnants of last season's asparagus stalks

What a work crew we are as we march
To our winter-worn patch
Singing it's off to work we go
Granpy and his grandson crew
Nick and cole and granpy
Gardeners still in pajamas
On this early spring morning
Granpy as old as dirt
You two so young and sweet
And covered with mud
How you must wonder as I examine
And point out each dead stalk
And new-grown weed
We work …
Our time so short together
Don't ask when you are going back home
Stay with me in our garden
And later we'll finish our pajama baseball world series game
it's still the bottom of the ninth
You'll never know how much
This morning means to me
Love,
Granpy

Melange

i've read the poems
in the pages of melange
and what did i find there waiting to be discovered
to be read and enjoyed and internalized
the poems from the kids at Tenney School
i read the pain of loss
of joy and sorrow
alice not knowing her mother
but believing in her just the same
more poems more stories
you made your words into photographs
and you put the world in there with you
moms and dads sisters brothers uncles
grammas granpas dogs cats baseball the patriots and much
more
you kids poured it all out
onto the pages of melange
poured out your hearts
your deepest feelings
your very beings
writing so simply about
the people and places and things
you really really love
i loved it so....

To Cassie

Keep writing about your father
write it all down day after day
write and write some more
write the things about your father you miss the most
drown yourself in your father's memory
keep the poems read the poems
go to his gravesite read the poems over and over again
and cry and cry and cry
and keep doing it for days and days
write a poem read the poem and cry some more until you
just can't stand it anymore
find keepsakes of your father and keep them
close to you his favorite shirt or baseball cap
hold his keys in your hand and sit in his car and talk to him
just like he was there with you
cuz his is and he always will be
sit in his favorite chair cook his favorite dish for supper
keep a photo of him with you in your
room on your dresser
keep his memory alive forever
and write letters to him
through your poetry
wring out the very last tear
like an old washcloth
twist it and turn it and watch
as the last teardrop rinses away forever
that's what you have to do
get to the last tear
for the last time
and then go out in the world we live in
and go out and touch somebody
someone sad just like you used to be
before you finally got that last tear out …
visit a woman in a nursing home
who would love to have you read
her a story and maybe some of your daddy's poems
so you could cry together

work with special kids who can't see
or hear or even walk
bring some of your self to them
give them some of your own special joy
there are people out there who need you
who want to meet you to talk to you
to love you …
they want a piece of you
give it to them … all of you now cuz
when you do you will finally realize
the last tear is finally gone

Dear Addie

Here are the instructions for getting to the
heartfelt part of poetry.

Write about what you know
about simple things ordinary things
and people and places and good times and bad times
it's not rocket science
write about people you love
people you have lost
people you want back in your life
so bad it hurts
write about special things that you do
places you love to visit to just sit in and surround yourself
with its beauty
write about the happy times
the walks to the barn with your dad
simple ordinary things
familiar things
things from memory
things filled with love
sometimes anger
and even sometimes hate
follow these instructions carefully
and you'll get to the heartfelt part of writing poetry
write about ordinary things
just try, my friend, to make them beautiful
remember a poem is like a photograph and when someone
reads it
they find themselves in the photo
right there beside you
in your beautiful poem

Old Men Crying
A Reading Glass Poem

I'm going to cry a lot
when I'm old
I cry now like the old men
I see crying
at the strangest
most peculiar times
they cry so quick
when memories spark images
the lips quiver and eyes moisten
old men cry so easily
I'm going to cry a lot too
when I'm old
Why do they
cry so easily?
They don't just cry
at weddings and funerals
they cry at the funniest
most peculiar times
those times when
love or heartbreak or history
which branded them in youth
comes back to them
at the strangest most peculiar times
they cry alone
or in a room filled with strangers
they cry in family time
at the silliest most peculiar things
these silly old men
these teary-eyed sages
who over the years
have seen it all
or so it seems

For why do they cry so easily?
so quick
so very strange
I'm going to cry a lot
when I'm old …

My New Life
Tony Marino III
December 14, 2007

Accomplishments come and go
Some live in a temporary memory
Others fade into the past like a train leaving a
Deserted station.
Gone.
But not you.
You came on a silent sunny Friday
So softly, so calmly, so beautiful.
You came to us as a gift, a treasure, a miracle
I can almost hear your innocent footsteps
As your heart beats inside her.
Tiny
Loving
Precious
Part of us
You are my purpose
You have my heart, my soul, my mind
You will break me down to create a new …
A new heart, a new soul, a new mind
My New Life
A Life I Will Always Love

Birth Announcement
A son, Maximus Antonio Marino,
to Jennifer and Tony Marino III
of Charlotte, N.C., on August 5, 2008

About the Author

A graduate of Holyoke High School in Holyoke, Massachusetts, Tony Marino attended Holyoke Community College and later was awarded a Bachelor of Arts degree in English from Westfield State College. Later he received a Master of Arts in Teaching from Salem State College and did further  graduate studies at the University of New Hampshire and Lesley University. He taught at Hampton Academy in Hampton, N.H., and later co-authored a book of poetry entitled *Chalk Dust* while teaching at Pentucket Middle School in West Newbury, MA. He also taught at North Hampton School in North Hampton, N.H., where he lives with his wife Diane.

Visit Tony's website at:
www.tonytheteacherpoet.com